A Guide to Hist
Scarborough

Scarborough Archaeological and Historical Society

Published on behalf of the Scarborough Community Heritage Initiative by the Scarborough Archaeological and Historical Society

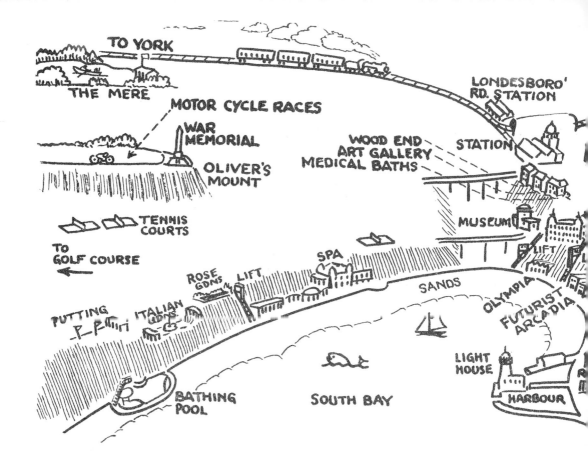

Scarborough's attractions circa 1960.

First published in the United Kingdom in 2003 by the Scarborough
Archaeological and Historical Society. Reprinted 2007.

10 Westbourne Park
Scarborough YO12 4AT

ISBN 0 902 41607 3

British Cataloguing in Publication Data.
A CIP catalogue record for this book is available from the British Library.

Designed by Robert Updegraff
Printed by Falcon Press (Stockton-on-Tees) Ltd.

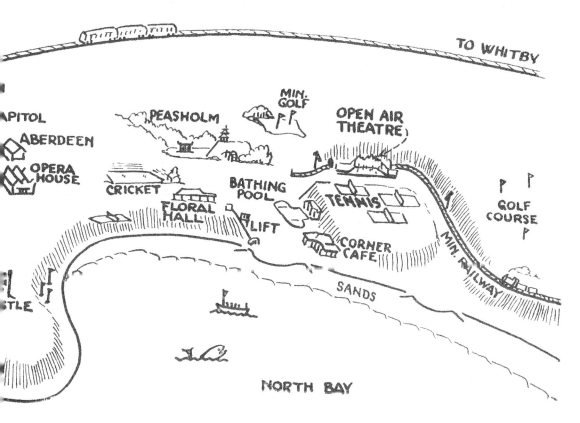

Contents

Foreword

I first came to Scarborough in the 1950s. I am deeply attached to the place and to the surrounding countryside. Over the years, of course, I have seen the disappearance of many fine buildings – sometimes of necessity; sometimes through sheer neglect. Rarely what arises in their place are improvements. It is easy to get depressed.

But this *Guide to Historic Scarborough* encourages you to see the town through fresh eyes. I always knew it was an interesting town; I knew a little about its history but it was only after reading this book that I became aware of what I'd missed. It's fascinating.

I congratulate the Community Heritage Initiative team, which has assembled the *Guide* with such care. It is short, succinct but very entertaining. I can't wait to get out now and explore for myself.

Sir Alan Ayckbourn
Scarborough
July 2003

Introduction

This *Guide to Historic Scarborough* is published by the Scarborough Archaeological and Historical Society as part of its Community Heritage Initiative (CHI) project. The project lasts for two years and is funded by the Local Heritage Initiative, a partnership between the Countryside Agency, the Heritage Lottery Fund and Nationwide Building Society, the purpose of which is to enhance knowledge, understanding and enjoyment of Scarborough's heritage. The book follows many years of research and excavation in the Old Town and elsewhere by members of the Scarborough Archaeological and Historical Society.

The *Guide* does not set out to be a comprehensive history of Scarborough. Rather, it reflects the enthusiasms and expertise of members of the CHI team, whose aim is to share their knowledge and encourage you to get out and explore the rich history and archaeology of the town. When you read this book you will discover that Scarborough, unlike many other seaside resorts, has a long and interesting history. For example, in the Middle Ages the herring trade made it one of the richest towns in the country, where fish were bought and sold on the sands for forty-five days each year at the original Scarborough Fair. Scarborough was Britain's first seaside resort, and the seaside holiday was invented here in the seventeenth century. Each of the book's nine chapters deals with an aspect of the town's history. At the end of the book are three walks, each with its own map, which take in some of the most visible features of Scarborough's past.

The writing, illustrating and production of this book was a collective effort made by volunteers from the Community Heritage Initiative team. The following people contributed their expertise to individual chapters: Anne Bayliss, Paul Bayliss, Jack Binns, Chris Evans, Chris Hall, Keith Johnston, Trevor Pearson, John Rushton and Faith Young. An executive committee made up of Farrell Burnett, Frances Hall, Keith Johnston and John Rushton supervised the writing and production of the book. Geoff Wood took many of the photographs. Other team members who contributed to the project were Jenny Kemp, Colin Langford, Madeleine Parkyn and Moyra Swan Fallows. Ray Mantell kindly photographed the cover painting at very short notice.

Special thanks are due to Bryan Berryman and the staff in the Scarborough Room of the Scarborough Public Library for unfailing helpfulness in locating illustrations and documents. We are also grateful to Jane Mee, Lara Goodband, David Buchanan, Karen Snowden and Laura Turner of the Scarborough Museums & Gallery for providing access to and information about their collections.

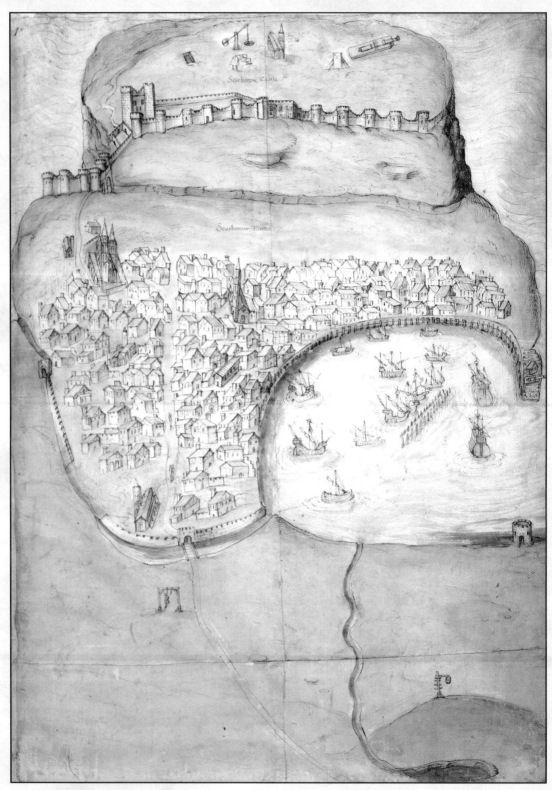

By the fifteenth century the town was in economic decline. This view of Scarborough, drawn about 1538 for military purposes, shows that the street plan of the town had still not extended beyond the medieval wall and ditch.

The development of the town

The way the town has grown and developed has reflected the rises and falls of its fortunes.

Why here?

The lie of the land, the need for defence, access to the necessities of life and lines of communication are all factors which influence where towns are founded, grow and succeed. The area that was to become Scarborough has what it takes to develop a successful town – there are good defensive positions, a sheltered bay where ships can come and go, and the sea itself to provide fish for food or for sale. Inland from Scarborough is varied countryside providing additional resources such as timber and stone. Most of all though, in the twelfth century the building of a royal castle and the founding of a borough helped to put Scarborough on the map and secure its position as one of the most successful towns in England.

Early settlers

The earliest inhabitants we know about lived on the castle headland in the early Iron Age, around 2,500 years ago. They may have had their round houses inside a hill fort with ramparts about where the outer wall of the Castle now stands. Although the Romans built a signal station, the foundations of which can be seen on the edge of the cliff inside the Castle's wall, there is very little evidence that they settled here. Archaeologists found some evidence of a small Roman settlement in 1999 near Castle Road behind the YMCA. The Roman road to the signal station probably ran

The extensive flat area of the castle headland could easily have held a large Iron Age hill fort. The steep slopes make the site easy to defend but there is access inland along the ridge where the entrance to the Castle now stands.

along the line of what is now Victoria Road and Castle Road, and this may have influenced the way the town was laid out in medieval times.

Legend has it that a settlement was founded here by the Vikings Thorgils Scarthi and Kormak about 966. We do not know exactly where their town might have been, but we are told by the Icelandic poet Snorri Sturlusson that it was burnt to the ground by Harald Hardrada of Norway, who landed at Scarborough in 1066 before being defeated by King Harold of England at the battle of Stamford Bridge. It is a good story but up to now there is no archaeological evidence to back it up – neither the Viking town nor evidence of its burning have yet been found.

Founding the town

The town as we now know it originated in a borough founded by Henry II in about 1163. This was a planned town, near to the Castle and St Mary's Church and, like many planned towns from Roman times to the twenty-first century, the streets were laid out in a grid pattern.

Such was the success of the new town that Henry II sanctioned an extension to the west. This was known as the New Borough, and the older part became known as the Old Borough. New Borough was also laid out as a grid, though this was not on the same alignment as the first one. The slightly curving form of the streets may reflect the lines of earlier field boundaries.

By the end of the fourteenth century the town had grown as far as the present Bar Street and North Street, where the New Borough ended in defensive ramparts. The town had been a great success. Norman kings taxed towns on the basis of their wealth, and at its peak Scarborough was ranked the nineteenth most wealthy town in England. After that, however, evidence suggests that the New Borough was not fully built up, so the growth of the town must have begun to slow.

The new streets of the early medieval town lie parallel to and at right angles to Castle Road. The medieval surveyors may have taken the Roman road as their starting point. Down by the harbour, modern Quay Street and Sandside were outside the planned town and grew spontaneously, while Cooks Row and part of St Sepulchre Street ran diagonally to the pattern. This may be because around here was a marsh to be avoided. Another theory is that this may be part of an older town – perhaps this is where the Vikings were, but archaeologists have not yet been able to prove it.

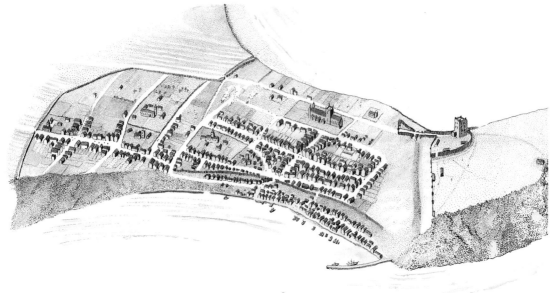

Building the early town

Although the grid pattern of the streets was easy to lay out, it was not a simple matter to build houses in Scarborough because of the steep slope downwards to the South Bay. A series of terracing walls had to be built, with level areas between them on which the buildings could stand.

Buildings of this period were mostly of timber, erected on top of stone footings. Stone-built houses were notable enough to merit special reference – John de Beverley built one 'by the Sandgate' between 1175 and 1194. Recent investigations at the Richard III House on Sandside suggest it may also be medieval in origin.

The two streets called East Sandgate and West Sandgate are probably the original links between the planned town and the harbour area. They both have sharp turns in them which may have marked the point where the road passed through the town defences.

The post-medieval town

By the fifteenth century, growth had ceased, and the town went into decline. Factors included the Black Death and the rise of Hull as a major rival.

Above Most of the terracing walls are not visible as they are under, or sometimes form part of, later buildings. This medieval terracing wall is still visible behind East Mount Flats, Longwestgate, a massively constructed stone wall at least four metres high. We know from archaeological work that there is another wall on the downhill side of Longwestgate, roughly parallel to this one.

Left This nineteenth-century drawing shows a medieval timber-framed house at Parkins Lane in Scarborough. The building was three storeys high with a two-bay gable overhanging Quay Street.

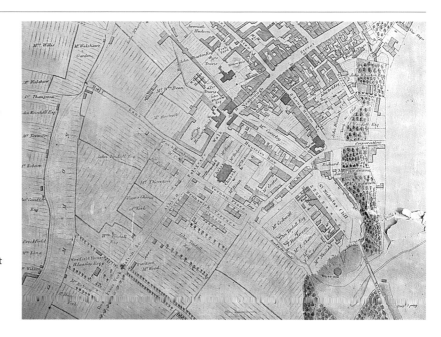

Right Expansion outside the defensive circuit did not really begin until the latter half of the eighteenth century and took place initially in the area of the present St Nicholas Cliff, Aberdeen Walk (shown here as Bull Lane) and Huntriss Row. This can be seen in John Wood's map of 1828.

Below This drawing by W. Tindall, published in 1832, shows the design for The Crescent as it was originally conceived: two substantial terraces to the north of an oval garden and seven linked villas to the south. A colonnaded pavillion proposed for the Valley was never built. This was town planning on the scale we normally associate with fashionable resorts, with a curving street, central gardens and a uniform terrace frontage, in complete contrast to the older part of the town.

The town expands again

In the eighteenth century the town began its second golden age, this time as a health and pleasure resort. Many buildings in the medieval town were redeveloped or simply had their appearance brought up to date with new facades.

In the early nineteenth century the town's popularity as a resort led to continued expansion. The building of the Spa Bridge in 1827 opened up the area south of the Valley, with both grand terraces, such as Esplanade or Crown Terrace, and smaller-scale housing for the grow-

ing middle-class population; an example would be Royal Crescent, which was laid out by Joseph Paxton, the architect of the Crystal Palace. In 1830 William and John Barry and John Uppleby acquired two large fields above the Valley from John Tindall, a Scarborough shipbuilder, and employed the York architects R.H. and Samuel Sharp to design and lay out the area we now know as The Crescent.

The railway arrived in Scarborough from York in 1845. Communications were vastly improved and the town expanded rapidly to the north, west and south. Many of the new purpose-built hotels, such as the Grand Hotel, were designed to be impressive. There were grand suburban houses for the rich middle classes and extensive areas of artisan housing, where many of the streets were laid out to a gridiron pattern – just like those in Henry II's town.

Modern growth

Scarborough's growth continued in the twentieth century. Much of this took place in suburbs well beyond the historic core of the town. Fingers of development spread out down Filey and Seamer Roads but the greatest expansion took place in the north at Peasholm, Northstead and Barrowcliff. In the words of historian Jack Binns, the town spread out and thinned out. Extensive clearance of sub-standard housing in the Old Town led to the loss of many of the 'yards' – blocks of terrace housing, many of them in the former gardens of earlier, larger houses. In 1921, the Scarborough Corporation bought the freehold of the royal manor of Northstead on which they built homes.

At the start of a new century, Scarborough continues to expand and looks forward to a new period of prosperity.

Council house building started at Edgehill and was followed by Prospect Mount, Barrowcliff and Northstead. The new estates were planned with wide roads, often curving or in crescents, and large gardens – very different from the Old Town with its grid of tightly built streets. This picture of Broadway on the Northstead Estate in 1940 shows the spacious design which was heavily influenced by the 'garden cities' ideal.

At the heart of the medieval castle is the tall stone keep, built by Henry II between 1158 and 1168. The keep contained the private rooms of the castle governor as well as a great hall for feasting and a chapel over the entrance. The keep is built on one side of a raised mound that is probably all that is left to see of an earlier castle built by William le Gros.

The defence of the town

The headland at Scarborough is one of the best defensive locations along the north-east coast of England. The town which developed under the headland was well protected by sea cliffs on both the north and south sides, but from prehistoric times onwards successive generations have improved its defences.

Hill-fort bay

The headland at Scarborough is now dominated by the ruins of the medieval castle begun by King Henry II about the year 1155, but archaeologists think the hill top was first fortified 2,500 years ago in the early Iron Age. Settlement remains dating from this era have been found on the summit and it is possible that the entire headland was a large fort defended by a rampart facing inland, about where the castle wall now runs. No trace of these fortifications has so far been found, but Scarborough might be the 'hill-fort bay' mentioned by the Roman geographer Ptolemy.

The excavated remains of a Roman watchtower dating from the end of the fourth century AD show up clearly in this aerial view. The Romans fortified the hill top by siting one of their chain of coastal watchtowers on the summit. It was intended to guard against sea-borne attackers, but was garrisoned only for thirty years before they withdrew from Britain. The foundations of the tower and part of the encircling ditch can still be seen perched on the edge of the cliff overlooking Marine Drive.

The medieval castle

The first castles were built in England soon after the Norman conquest of 1066, but it was not until 1135 that a local baron called William le Gros built the first castle at Scarborough. It was sited on the headland and probably consisted of an artificial mound or motte with an encircling timber palisade and a tall wooden tower in the centre. It lasted for only twenty years before King Henry II took over the site and began work on the present castle. Other medieval kings then added to the castle defences to create one of the most powerful royal fortresses in the north of England.

The medieval town defences

Scarborough has never been better protected than in the medieval period with the Castle on the headland and defences to protect the weaker sides of the town. Compared to the medieval walls of York or the castle battlements, the town defences were fairly modest and there are almost no traces left to see. There was a stone wall on the south side of the town overlooking the harbour while on the west side, facing inland, there were two successive lines of defences. The first was built to enclose the Old Borough, which was the first settlement established by Henry II. These defences stretched all the way between the South and North Bays.

In 1989 remains of the Old Borough ditch unexpectedly came to light during building works in Leading Post Street at the back of the Market Hall. Volunteers, including local schoolchildren, had just hours to investigate the site before it was built over. The town later expanded outside the Old Borough ditch with the creation of the New Borough, and a new line of defences was built further to the west aligned along what is now Bar Street, North Street and Castle Road. The only section of the medieval town wall still standing is on Castle Road and probably dates from the late fifteenth century. After the Old Borough ditch had gone out of use, it became a convenient place to dump rubbish. Among the remains unearthed by archaeologists in 1989 was the almost-complete skeleton of a horse.

Newborough Gate

The gate into the New Borough, known as Newborough Bar, was the main entrance into Scarborough. It stood across the shopping street we now know as Newborough, near the entrance to Bar Street. There were other town gates as well in Castle Road and above the harbour at East Sandgate and West Sandgate. Newborough Bar is the only entrance about which very much is known. It was probably constructed in the second half of the twelfth century as part of the defences around the New Borough. In the medieval period there was a wide ditch in front of the gate crossed by a drawbridge; beyond it, open fields stretched away to the village of Falsgrave. There is no picture of the gate until the 1530s, when it was over three hundred years old. It was a rather squat, ugly building with a single arched opening and a line of battlements on top, not at all like the elegant

After the old gate was demolished, a new gate was built in 1843 in the then-fashionable Gothic style with mock battlements between two corner turrets. Unlike its predecessor, the last gate to stand at the top of Newborough was never intended for serious defence. At last Scarborough had a gateway to rival those of York, but after only forty-seven years it was demolished as a traffic hazard and never replaced.

In the Second World War the town was attacked from the air more than twenty times. The worst bombing occurred on the night of 18 March 1941 when an estimated 1,000 incendiary bombs fell on the town. More than two dozen people were killed and over 1,300 buildings were damaged around the town. This photograph, taken the day after the raid, shows the resulting devastation of the Old Town. After the war several buildings had to be replaced entirely and some sites remained vacant for many years.

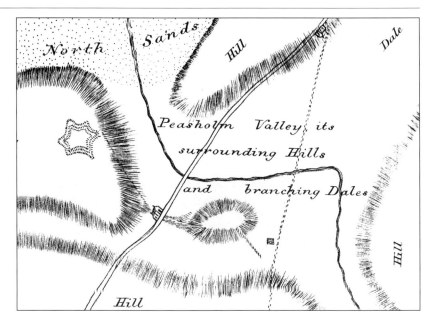

This map from 1855 shows the Civil War star fort at Peasholm. Another fort on the South Bay was totally destroyed when the Esplanade Hotel was built in the nineteenth century. These star forts overlooked and defended Peasholm Gap and the vulnerable points where sea-borne troops might land. Star shaped to provide maximum crossfire, they are precursors to the pill boxes of later conflicts. Part of the Peasholm fort was excavated in 1991 when ditches and musket balls were found.

turreted medieval gates still to be seen at York. From medieval times until the nineteenth century, Newborough Bar served as the town prison, leading the author of one guidebook to observe in 1796, 'at Scarborough the approach to health, pleasure and delight is under the arch of misery, and, we trust, repentance!'.

The Civil War

Scarborough's defences were never seriously tested until the English Civil War when the town was the scene of military activity. It was besieged for three weeks by parliamentary forces. When the final assault came on 18 February 1645, the parliamentarians soon broke through to capture the town.

Invasion scares

The last time the town's medieval defences were prepared for war was in 1745 when Scarborough feared attack by the Scottish forces of Bonnie Prince Charlie. A committee was appointed 'to put this town in a posture of defence against the rebels' and it set workmen to dig out the old New Borough ditch and ring the town with gun batteries, using ninety-nine cannon brought from ships in the harbour. A force of 800 was deployed to man the defences but thankfully their valour was never tested as the Scottish army chose an invasion route to the west of the Pennines. Scarborough still felt vulnerable to a foreign invasion and at intervals thereafter volunteer forces were raised to defend the town. In 1798 the town had five companies of infantry amounting to 400 men and a troop of cavalry. Resplendent in their red uniforms and proudly bearing the town crest on their silk banner, they were never called upon to do anything more dangerous than man the gun batteries at the Castle.

New threats

The twentieth century saw Scarborough attacked from the air and bombarded from the sea while the Castle continued to play an important role in defending this stretch of coastline. At the start of the First World War there was a coastguard look-out station on the edge of the castle cliff on exactly the same site as the Romans' watchtower 1,700 years before. In a bungalow next to the coastguard station operators used a secret naval listening device to detect submarines off the coast. Both were damaged by shelling on 16 December 1914 when the German navy bombarded the Castle and town for half an hour,

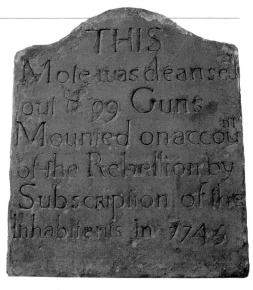

killing 17 and injuring over 80. The attack sparked fears of an imminent invasion and prompted a major recruiting drive for the army under the banner 'Remember Scarborough'.

Scarborough's defences against a sea-borne invasion in the Second World War included barbed wire and anti-tank obstacles along the seafront and a small defence battery at Peasholm Gap on the North Side. On the South Side at Wheatcroft, there was a battery of powerful breech-loading naval guns dating from the First World War. These were capable of firing six-inch shells far out to sea and over into the North Bay. Thankfully, the guns were never fired in anger.

Over the centuries, Scarborough has adapted to changing patterns of warfare. Now the defence of the town is conducted from a distance and determined by national, not local, needs.

Above The so-called Mote Stone, now in the Rotunda Museum, was found in the ditch near Newborough Bar and commemorates the deployment of ninety-nine guns to defend the town during the invasion scare of 1745. Six of these guns were positioned immediately outside Newborough Bar to fire up the street we now know as Westborough. The inscription on the stone reads 'THIS Mote was cleansed out & 99 Guns Mounted on account of the Rebellion by Subscription of the Inhabitants In 1745.'

Left In order to protect vulnerable points from sea-borne landings, defences such as pill boxes and anti-aircraft emplacements were built in Cayton Bay and Scalby Nab. This pill box in the North Bay survived until 1961. The island behind it, which gives it some protective cover, was known as Monkey Island. The island and the pill box were removed in the 1960s to make way for the new sea wall.

Development of Scarborough's harbour

1565–present

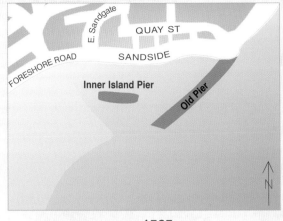

pre-1565

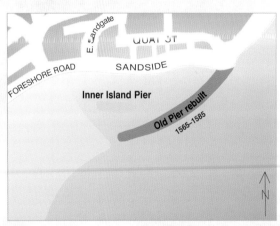

1565–1732

1732–1746

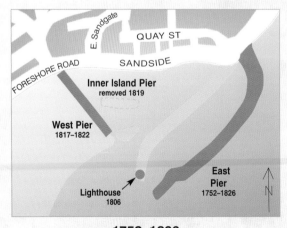

1752–1826

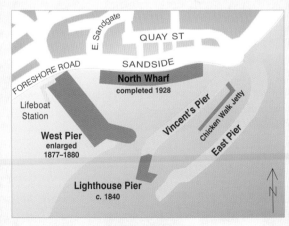

1840–present

These maps, based on contemporary drawings but not drawn to scale, indicate how Scarborough's harbour has developed over the centuries. Monarchs and engineers alike have poured time, money and effort into transforming the Scarborough 'peers' of 1565 to what they are today. Materials such as timber, iron and stone have been used during construction, and present-day technology is now being used to continue the preservation of an important and busy harbour. ▬ = New construction ▬ = Previous construction

Scarborough's harbour

The history of Scarborough's harbour can be traced back to medieval times. Through the subsequent centuries, its importance has waxed and waned, but it has always featured in the development of the town.

The early harbour

Although a pier probably already existed, Henry III granted Scarborough the right to construct a new port 'with timber and stone' in 1252. Ships could then safely sail in and out at both high and low water. The harbour was paid for by tolls, or quayage, imposed upon both sea-borne trade and fishing. A merchant ship paid six shillings, a fisherman's ship four shillings and a fisherman's boat two shillings.

Recent excavations at The Bolts and Quay Street have uncovered evidence of the medieval harbour area. Domestic refuse was deliberately dumped to consolidate land behind the quay. This helped support the quay wall, protecting Scarborough's early waterfront from the North Sea tides, and allowed land to be gradually reclaimed from the sea's grasp for building. Mooring rings have been found in the basements of properties along Quay Street, suggesting the location of the earlier harbour.

Archaeologists have discovered well-preserved fish remains, including the bones of haddock, in excavations on Quay Street. During medieval times, fish featured heavily in the daily diet. Herring were harvested off Scarborough during the late summer and early autumn months and, once caught, they needed to be preserved. During the twelfth century, these fish had only enough salt sprinkled on them to prepare them for immediate sale; by the fourteenth century, the practice was to gut and salt them and sprinkle extra salt between the layers of fish, and then pack them head-to-tail into tightly sealed barrels. This was more or less the method used until the middle of the twentieth century by the herring fleets and their followers, the 'herring girls', whose job it was

Medieval recipe for herring

'First broil them very brown, then have ready some white-wine made hot with an Anchovy, a blade of Mace, and a bit of Onion, with a little whole Pepper, all stew'd in the Wine, then cut off the heads of the fish, and braise them in the wine and spice, and take them out again before you put in your Herrings; let them stew over Coals, in a Dish that they may lie at length in; let them stew on both sides, 'till they are enough at the Bone; take them out, and shake up the Sauce with the Butter and Flower.

'Tis a very good Way to Dress them.'

to gut the fish and prepare them for transport. They worked long back-breaking hours with skill and dexterity: seasoned workers could gut a fish a second, using a tool called the gipping knife. These women became something of a tourist attraction in Scarborough and were much photographed.

The construction of the piers

The poor state of the harbour's stone and timber pier (the Old Pier) was brought to the attention of Henry VIII. In 1546 not only users of the harbour but also property owners in the area had to contribute towards its upkeep. In response to a petition, Elizabeth I in 1565 granted royal aid in the form of cash, timber and iron for the rebuilding of the 800-foot long and 20-foot wide Old Pier. Earlier in the sixteenth century, another smaller pier (later called the Inner Island Pier) had been constructed on the landward side of the Old Pier; it was in use until 1819, when it was demolished. The harbour still needed constant upkeep. During the English Civil War, ships were lost, buildings damaged, trade was adversely affected and piracy rife.

Archaeologists have discovered medieval timber work in the former public house called the Three Mariners on Quay Street and also in the Newcastle Packet public house on Sandside. Historical documents from the period indicate that high rents were paid along this route, suggesting that the hub of medieval life was in this area. Wandering along these two streets, one can see the uneven and zigzag shape of the cobbled path following the earlier quay alignment.

Very little improved in the harbour until after the 1732 and 1752 Acts of Parliament which paved the way for major construction. The Acts sought to make more effective use of tolls laid upon vessels carrying coal and other cargoes from the port of Newcastle Upon Tyne to London, using Scarborough harbour as a place of refuge on the long journey.

Several engineers worked on the Old Pier over the years, including William Lelam, who proposed building an extension to it in the 1730s. This arm was later separated from the main body of the Old Pier by an opening called Pet Hole, thus creating the Outer Island Pier. This later became part of West Pier. In the 1740s, William Vincent took over the work on the Old Pier, which was extended further southwards. Over time, the Old Pier became known as Vincent's Pier, work on which was completed by 1746.

The increasing revenue created from the tolls and the development of offshore shipping allowed an outer pier to be constructed, outside the stretch of Vincent's Pier, so that the main harbour was protected from weather and tides. Ideas were submitted by John Smeaton, the great civil engineer who was famous for constructing the third Eddystone Lighthouse south-west of Plymouth. In 1753 work began on what came to be called the East Pier. It took 76 years to build and used about 140,000 tons of stone.

William Chapman's 1831 drawing of the harbour area.

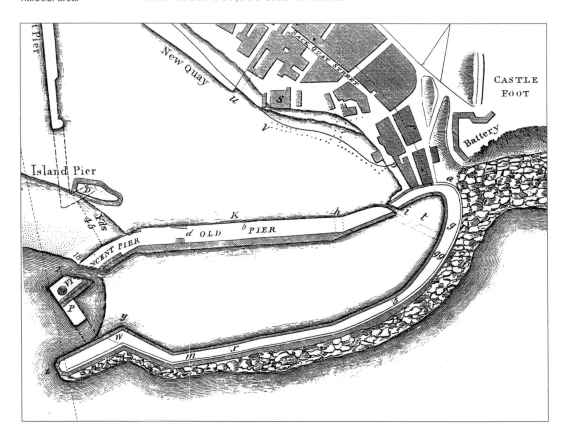

With the 'discovery' of the 'Spaw' in the South Bay in 1626, Scarborough began to attract many wealthy tourists. Fishing, although a steady source of trade, was not as successful or important as in previous centuries and families of fishermen were at times in hardship. In 1682, the first Trinity House Hospital was built on St Sepulchre Street, which offered health care to needy seamen and their families. In addition, in 1747, the Scarborough Merchant Seamen's Hospital was built on a site near the top of Auborough Street and in 1832 the current Trinity House was constructed, replacing the previous two institutions.

Between 1840 and 1852, Vincent's Pier was extended to form the shape it bears today. An opening cut obliquely through the masonry divided the pier into two parts. The smaller pier is often referred to as Lighthouse Pier, and is connected to the main part of Vincent's Pier by a mechanised drawbridge.

West Pier, designed by William Chapman, was completed in 1822. It was subsequently lengthened between 1877 and 1880, and also incorporated the Outer Island Pier which had originally been constructed in the 1700s. In 1826, the foundation was laid for Corporation Wharf which was gradually built up to form the North Wharf, completed in 1928.

Trinity House and the Merchant Seamen's Hospital

Trinity House Hospital originally provided medical help for needy local fishing families and for those who had served on Scarborough-based ships. The Society of Owners, Masters and Mariners, founded in 1602, provided financial backing through voluntary contributions for the original Trinity House Hospital. In 1747, an Act of Parliament created the Merchant Seamen's Fund which required Scarborough's ship owners and masters to pay sixpence a month for every crew member during his time in service. These proceeds helped to finance the construction of the Scarborough Merchant Seamen's Hospital (later demolished).

Shipbuilding in Scarborough

Between 1771 and 1820, 155 ships were launched from Tindall's yard. Tindall Street, off Victoria Road, is named after the family. One of the Tindall shipyard's apprentices was William Harland, who later co-founded the famous Harland & Wolff shipyards at Belfast.

The wars in which Great Britain was involved in the late eighteenth and early nineteenth centuries greatly aided the local shipping industry. Many vessels were used in the wartime transport service. During the American War of Independence, the entire shipping stock of Tindall's shipyard was commandeered. Tindall's was the largest of several yards and was situated on Sandside. Other shipyards existed below the present-day location of the Grand Hotel and on the site of the Olympia Amusement Arcade.

Scarborough's lifeboat

Scarborough's first lifeboat was launched in 1801, built by local boat builder Charles Smith. The Royal National Lifeboat Institution, founded in 1824, did not take over the Scarborough station until 1861. The lifeboat house occupied two other sites before it moved to its present location adjacent to the West Pier: the first, near Beck Mill (underneath the Spa Bridge where the present Valley Road joins the Foreshore); the second, opposite its current location, and now part of the Silver Dollar amusement arcade. Finally, the Royal National Lifeboat Institution took over its current location in 1940.

The harbour in the late nineteenth and twentieth centuries

The late nineteenth and twentieth centuries were periods of change for the local fishing industry. Trawling vessels had arrived in Scarborough in the 1830s. The arrival of the York to Scarborough railway in 1845 encouraged inland transport of fish, particularly to West Yorkshire. Steam trawlers appeared in the harbour by the 1870s. Methods of fishing, such as long-lining, were used in Scarborough until the late twentieth century along with trawling, although the two methods did not always exist together harmoniously. Fishing was still profitable enough to finance the construction of a new fish market in 1961. However, fish stocks have dwindled over the generations, and fishermen today are strictly limited by European Commission Total Allowable Catches.

Today, leisure boats can moor in the basin between the East Pier and Vincent's Pier. The Chicken Walk Jetty gives easy access to the vessels. In the main harbour, boats such as the *Coronia* and *Regal Lady* provide sightseeing trips for visitors and locals. If ships need repairing, the dry dock grid, visible at low tide and located on the inside wall of Vincent's Pier, allows ships to rest out of water and undergo repairs.

The history of Scarborough's harbour is one of an almost constant struggle to improve and maintain the quays and piers, which are vulnerable to attack by the sea and to decay. In the first part of the twenty-first century further reinforcements to the East Pier – rock armour and accropodes – became necessary to ensure that it could continue to serve its purpose.

Bombarded on 16 December 1914, at the beginning of the First World War, the damage to Scarborough's lighthouse is clearly visible. It was demolished three days later, and was not fully rebuilt until 1931. The piers were relatively unscathed, but there was extensive damage to residential areas in the town. The first lighthouse, a round brick tower with railings encircling its flat top, was constructed in 1806. A coal fire burned on top originally, but in later years a copper reflector was installed to reflect the light out to sea.

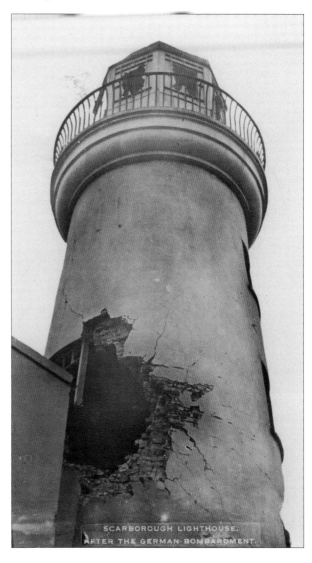

SCARBOROUGH LIGHTHOUSE,
AFTER THE GERMAN BOMBARDMENT.

The damage done to Sr Mary's during the sieges of the Castle in 1645 and 1648, when the church was used as a forward artillary post by Parliament's soldiers, is still visible today. The post-Civil War church is much smaller than its medieval predecessor, which was as grand and as large as a cathedral.

Religion in Scarborough

Scarborough has had a long, lively and important religious history.

During the Middle Ages, when England was part of the universal or Catholic Church of western Europe, Scarborough had many religious buildings. In addition to the parish church, St Mary's, which still survives, there were two dependent chapels dedicated to St Thomas the Martyr and the Holy Sepulchre, and also the friaries of the Franciscans, Dominicans and Carmelites. Modern street names like Friars Gardens and Friars Way remind us of the former presence of the Dominicans, as also do archaeological remains. Window tracery from the Dominican friary was discovered recently when the Castle Hotel in Queen Street was redeveloped as a block of flats – Blackfriar House.

In an age when there was a widespread fear of the dreadful punishments of hell, people were very concerned about the fate of their souls, and also the souls of their relatives and friends. This was reflected in the existence of several chantry chapels in the town, where priests said masses for the souls of the dead. A skeleton recently unearthed on the cliff top near Mulgrave Place is thought to have been buried in one of these chapels dedicated to St Mary Magdalen.

The antiquarian John Leland, who visited the town in 1539, wrote that St Mary's was 'very faire and is isled on the sides, and crosse isled, and hath 3 auncient towres for belles with pyramides on them: whereof 2 toures be at the west end of that chirch, and one yn the midle of the cross isle'. This reconstruction shows St Mary's at its most magnificent, much as Leland must have seen it.

Religion was also of central importance in people's earthly lives. As early as 1200, Scarborough had at least two hospitals, St Thomas, for the care of paupers, and St Nicholas, a refuge for lepers. Later, several more almshouses for the poor were founded such as 'Goddeshouse' in Paradise, the enclosed garden area to the south-east of St Mary's which is still known by this name.

In addition, the friars provided the townspeople with chapels, confessors, preachers, and cemeteries. The Franciscans brought down clean water from Falsgrave springs by underground aqueduct and both they and the Dominicans paved streets.

Lay people had many opportunities to participate in the religious life of the town. Scarborough had several religious guilds in the later Middle Ages, for example those of St James, St George and St Nicholas. These were voluntary associations which raised money to maintain an altar dedicated to a particular saint, and sometimes a priest who would pray at the altar for the souls of the members. They did good works, enjoyed an annual feast, and ensured members a good turn-out at their funerals. Lay people could also take part in processions. The town's rulers were expected to set a good example by regular attendance at church.

There were at times frictions between lay people and clergy and between members of the clergy. One Dominican friar was assaulted by three local priests 'so that he despaired of his life'. But generally the church had an integrating effect upon the community. The importance of religion is shown by the fact that in their wills many people left money or goods for religious purposes. St Mary's Church received a large amount of jewels and other precious items, partly for use in services and partly for decoration. Robert Rillington, whose criminal record included treason in wartime as well as robbery, left two ships to pay for prayers for his soul.

The sixteenth-century Reformation

The number of religious buildings decreased when the friaries and the chantry chapels disappeared during the reigns of Henry VIII and Edward VI. Religious life became less visually colourful as emphasis switched from the mass to the sermon.

There was still a close link between ecclesiastical and secular authorities. People were expected to observe the official religion, Protestant now rather than Catholic, and to go to church regularly. They could be fined if they were absent or if they otherwise flouted the Sunday observance laws. When Archbishop Grindal's inspection of the parish took place in 1575, many people were accused of missing services, including some of the town's most important citizens, Bailiff Roberte Lacie among them. Some of them may have been Catholics at heart; others may simply have resented being told what to do.

By the 1630s, however, few Scarborians were breaking the rules regarding behaviour on Sundays. This decade also saw pews installed in St. Mary's, something that was highly desirable in an age of long sermons. However, there were only enough pews for the richer half of the community, those whose conformity in religion the authorities were most anxious to monitor.

Even before the Civil War, the fabric of St Mary's, which was as grand and as large as a cathedral, had begun to decay. The western towers were permanently dismantled after being badly damaged in a gale. As a result of the Civil War, it lost most of its chancel, north aisle, north transept and central bell tower. Only the last was later rebuilt after it had crashed down on the nave roof.

Still, the parish church fared better than the chapel of St Thomas which was used as a horse stable and military storehouse, its timber and slates looted 'by evill disposed persons'. It was pulled down and some of its stone piers 'imployed about the repairing of St Maryes church'.

The view of St Mary's familiar to generations of Scarborians and visitors, who have climbed the hillside from the Old Town to attend services.

Greater religious diversity after the Civil War

The unity and monopoly of the established Church of England was destroyed in the mid-seventeenth century, and during the centuries that followed Scarborians were to witness the development of Nonconformist groups which was so successful that the Anglicans found themselves outnumbered by Christians of other denominations.

A small group of Quakers existed in Scarborough when George Fox first visited the town in 1651. The Quakers outraged established belief and practice by refusing to attend church, pay its tithes or swear oaths, even of allegiance to the Crown, and as a result suffered decades of persecution and punishment. Nevertheless, Scarborough's small but distinguished group of Friends, with family names such as Bland, Tindall, Rowntree and Dennis, played leading parts in the town's commerce, education and charity during the next three centuries.

Baptists and Presbyterians also prospered, but the religious group with the strongest and widest popular appeal was the Methodists. John Wesley first rode into Scarborough in 1759; he revisited the town at least twelve times during the next thirty-two years in order to preach his message. He described the chapel in Church Steps Stairs as 'one of the neatest and most elegant preaching-houses in England', but with

Above George Fox, the founder of the Society of Friends, was imprisoned in Scarborough Castle from May 1665 to September 1666. Despite suffering cruel conditions during his time in the Castle, where his cell was exposed to open weather, he impressed the governor and soldiers there with his courage, friendliness and forbearance.

Right William Hannay, who was minister of the Presbyterian meeting house on St Sepulchre Street from 1703 to 1725, brought his Scottish father's Covenanter's Bible with him to Scarborough. The torn pages in the Bible show where it was pierced by a trooper's sword when Hannay's father was hiding in a barn in Scotland. The book remained in the meeting house, which eventually became Congregationalist, until its closure in 1928.

Above The colourful pulpit in St-Martin-on-the-Hill displays the work of prominent Pre-Raphaelite artists, such as Dante Gabriel Rossetti who painted the Annunciation on the side panels.

Left The development of the South Cliff, which attracted rich visitors willing to contribute to the expense, saw the building of some spectacular churches. St Martin's Anglican Church is a Pre-Raphaelite masterpiece by Bodley with decoration by Morris and Co. Not to be outdone, the Nonconformists built in triumphant Gothic style — the Wesleyans at South Cliff Methodist and the Congregationalists at St. Andrew's. The latter, shown here, has been called a cathedral of nonconformity because of its size.

space for fewer than 300 people it soon proved to be too small for the town's rapidly growing Methodist community. One local nineteenth-century commentator declared that 'Wesleyan Methodism may be said to grip the town at all points'. The chapel in Queen Street, opened in 1840, had seating for about 1,600 people but frequently accommodated nearly 2,000 worshippers.

There was great enthusiasm also for Primitive Methodism. When William Clowes first came to Scarborough, the 'preaching room' at 4 Globe Street proved too small for all those who wished to hear him so instead he addressed 'a prodigious mass of hearers, more than could hear me' on the South Bay sands. Other open-air meetings were held on the castle dykes. The first Primitive Methodist chapel in the town was a 'home-made' structure erected by local fishermen in 1821. It was well used with sermons on Sundays and Fridays, prayer meetings on Mondays and Wednesdays, and fellowship groups on Thursdays.

In response to the Nonconformist challenge, the Anglicans shook off their complacent lethargy and were fired with evangelical zeal. Two new churches were opened in the early nineteenth century, one for 'the politer parts of the town' called Christ Church in Vernon Road, and the other, 'chiefly for the accommodation of the poor', St Thomas' in East Sandgate. St Mary's was renovated and 'purified' between 1848 and 1850 and many more free places provided.

Visitors participated in the church parades that were a feature of Sunday mornings on both the South and North Cliffs, sometimes beginning well before the actual services finished. This suggests a form of 'respectability religion' that contrasts with the intense belief in sin and providence held by many contemporaries.

With all the church and chapel building that was taking place, Theakston's first guidebook of 1840 could declare 'probably no town in the empire, of the same size, possesses a greater number of places for worship of God than Scarborough.'

Religious enthusiasm could lead to intolerance. When the Archbishop of York visited the town in 1850 he referred to 'the abominations of papal Rome', perhaps alarmed at the growing number of Catholics in Scarborough. There were divisions about education and about the new public cemetery. However, there could also be cooperation. The Bethel on Sandside, a place of religious worship

for sailors and fishermen, had non-denominational services attended by Baptists, Methodists, Presbyterians and Independents.

The Quaker Meeting House on Woodlands Drive.

As the town spread, new religious buildings were constructed on the outskirts, including St Luke's in Scalby Road, St Joseph's in Newby (by the eminent architect Francis Johnson) and the Quaker Meeting House on Woodlands Drive, indicating that there was still a real demand for church services.

Scarborians witnessed much church and chapel building in the nineteenth century. However, attendance at religious services fell in the twentieth century and some churches and chapels were demolished, including Christ Church, while others were made redundant and sold. Fewer people may attend church regularly, but there are many active Christians for whom religion is a key part of their lives.

Scarborough at the start of the twenty-first century contains a range of lively and active Christian communities, including the Church of Latter-Day Saints and the Salvation Army.

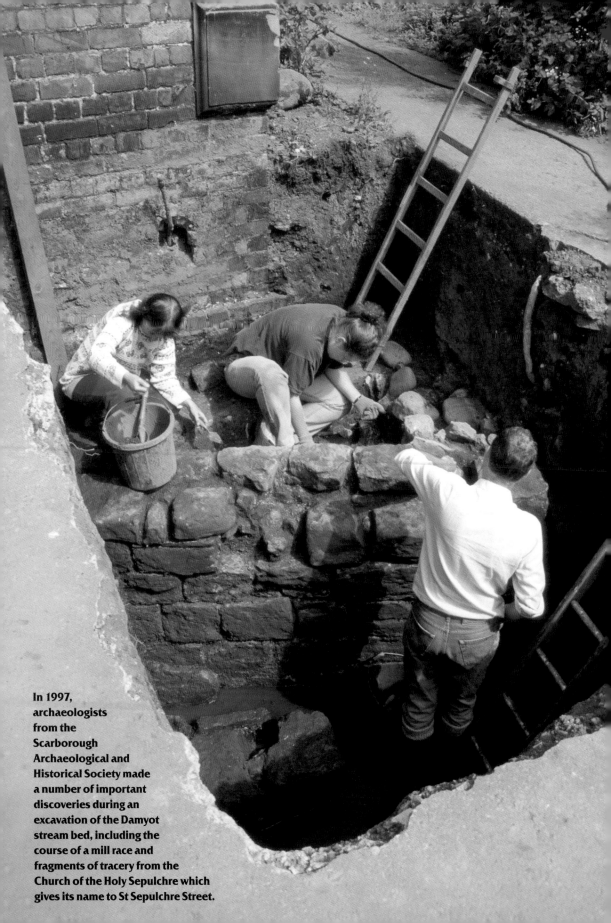

In 1997, archaeologists from the Scarborough Archaeological and Historical Society made a number of important discoveries during an excavation of the Damyot stream bed, including the course of a mill race and fragments of tracery from the Church of the Holy Sepulchre which gives its name to St Sepulchre Street.

Water for Scarborough

Salt water brought fish, merchandise and visitors to Scarborough; by contrast, lack of sufficient fresh water played a major role in the town's history. From medieval times to more recent years, Scarborians have struggled ingeniously to meet the challenge of maintaining a supply of fresh water for the town's increasing population.

Wells: The earliest water sources

There are now three wells in existence on the castle headland, and it is likely that one of these served the Roman signal station. Two wells are close to the Chapel of Our Lady on the cliff edge, although one of these is set within a vault holding an eighteenth-century water tank. The third, located in the inner bailey of the Castle's keep, is over 150 feet deep. The headland wells played an important role during the Civil War, when royalists in the Castle were besieged from below by parliamentarians. The existence of the wells, and the springs at the foot of the headland, allowed the royalists to hold out for months during the Great Siege of 1645. However, as the parliamentarian bombardment of the Castle intensified in the summer months, neither the bailey well nor the Chapel of Our Lady well provided enough water and it was no longer safe to draw from the springs at the bottom of the cliff. The shortage of water led to much disease and suffering for humans and animals and contributed to the royalist surrender.

Scarborough's early wells may have looked like this one taken from a view of Scarborough, drawn about 1538.

The town was served by other wells. The Borough well (probably fed by the Damyot stream) was at the east end of St Sepulchre Street. Another was 'behind the house called Paradise', not far from St Mary's Church. The well near the Chapel of Our Lady on the castle headland and the Paradise well contained water which was noted for its clarity. Because it was relatively free from unwanted solids, it weighed an ounce less per gallon than that from other wells. Townspeople continued to use the wells until the mid-nineteenth century.

The Damyot

The other important source of water for the medieval town was the stream called the Damyot (sometimes referred to as the Damgeth), which rose in Albemarle Crescent and flowed into the sea near the Lifeboat House. It supplied water for both domestic and industrial uses. In one of a series of excavations carried out between 1996 and 1998, the Scarborough Archaeological and Historical Society discovered a stone-lined portion of the Damyot's course to the east of

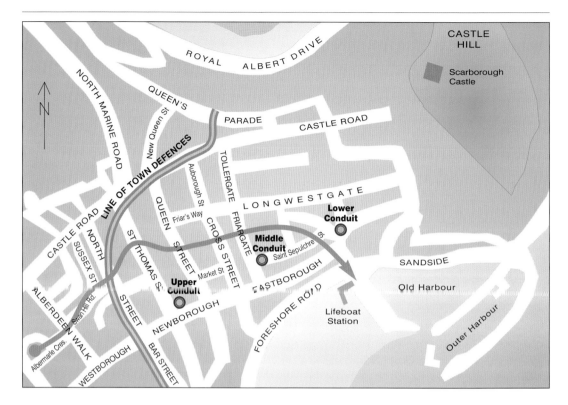

The Damyot (shown in blue) now runs in a culvert parallel to and north of Westborough before turning south near St Sepulchre Street and entering the sea near the Lifeboat House. It has yielded important finds to archaeologists interested in medieval life because the waterlogged ground along its course preserves organic material such as wood and leather which usually rot. The origin of the name may come from the Old Norse dammr, meaning dam, and geyt, meaning gushing spring or stream. Medieval Scarborough had three conduits to three troughs: Low, Middle and Upper. By the nineteenth century, these channels were insufficient and 'scenes of disorder, contention, turmoil, trouble and often fights' were reported as inhabitants crowded round the troughs to draw water.

Springfield. This may be the location of the mill operated by Reginald the Miller in the thirteenth century. We know from historical records that Reginald granted land on either side of the Damyot near the cemetery of the Church of the Holy Sepulchre to 'the Commonality of Scardburgh, to support the Friars dwelling and serving God there'. Although the stream has run underground in a culvert probably since the early nineteenth century, it has on occasion suddenly reappeared after times of heavy rainfall, most recently in August 2002. On 6 August 1857 it emerged and

> *rushed in torrents into Aberdeen Walk … choked up the Gullies in Queen's Street near Mrs Milson's Castle Hotel, thence under the archway, knocked down a garden wall on the premises, drowning and washing away a number of her pigs …*

The Damyot, which was a convenient place for medieval people to throw rubbish, soon became polluted. The stream and the wells, in any case, were unable to meet the needs of a growing town.

The Franciscan conduits

In 1283, Robert of Scarborough, Dean of York, proposed bringing water from springs and wells in what is now Falsgrave Park (then called Gildhuscliff) to the Franciscan friary and to the town. His plan was not realised until 1319, when water was brought to a trough known as the Middle Conduit which stood on the corner of Friargate

38

and St Sepulchre Street. The water then flowed to the Low Conduit at the other end of St Sepulchre Street, where the Butter Cross now stands. The two troughs soon proved inadequate and in 1339 the Franciscans built the Upper Conduit on the corner of St Thomas Street and Newborough. We know little about the nature and courses of the medieval water channels. Confusingly, the channels, the pipes through which water flowed and the end access troughs are all referred to as 'conduits' in the historical records. From time to time the medieval channels are uncovered. In 1932, when the block of shops and houses in Market Way was being built, a section of the conduit approximately 30 to 40 feet long was exposed. It ran parallel to the north wall of the Market Hall in the direction of the presumed location of the Franciscan friary. In the words of its discoverer, Mr A.H. Poole, the conduit 'was fully enclosed; the inside would be 10 to 11 inches square; formed of roughly hewn stone slabs 15 to 16 inches square and about 2 inches thick.' In 1968 and 1975 parts of the conduits were exposed on the northern side of Falsgrave Road near the turning to Scalby Road.

This eighteenth-century building covers a spring head in the north-east corner of Falsgrave Park. Earlier spring heads no longer visible were located at the bottom of the park near the top of Oak Road. Springhill in local street names commemorates the origin of the water the conduits brought to Scarborough.

The stone conduits were eventually replaced by lead pipes, probably laid within them. The minutes of Scarborough Corporation indicate that improvements were made to them in the first half of the seventeenth century. The pipes ran along Falsgrave Road, or in the King's Close which lay between Falsgrave Road and Londesborough Road. They required frequent repair. In 1628 Scarborough Corporation stipulated that ' ... every inhabitant shall fynd a sufficient laboring man to bare and digg upp the conduit pipes from Newbrough gate to the conduit head and to cover it agayne, and for want of sutch laborer to pay every tyme 6d to the sayd woork.'

Three cisterns were built at the Low, Middle and Upper conduits so that water levels could build up in times of light use and thus supply water during times of heavy use. In 1634 a decree commanded that the Middle Conduit should be covered with a locked trap door, only to be opened between six o'clock in the morning and six o'clock in the evening.

Victorian engineering comes to the rescue

By the early part of the nineteenth century, the conduit system originally built by the Franciscans, and modified by later generations, was inadequate to supply a growing resort town. The Scarborough Corporation considered a variety of schemes to increase the supply of water. The advice of Robert King, the Pickering surveyor who was also surveyor of Washington DC from 1797 to 1803, was sought, as was that of William Smith, the pioneer geologist. Smith recommended that 'the largest covered reservoir in England' be dug in what is now Chapman's Yard in Waterhouse Lane. A stone-lined reservoir was found by archaeologists here in 2002. Later, Smith's advice was invaluable, for his geological work suggested that a large aquifer (rock holding a reservoir of water) lay under the Vale of Pickering, to the west of Scarborough. This aquifer was tapped at the springs which fed Cayton Mill, on the beach at Cayton Bay, in 1845.

The water was pumped to the reservoir on the corner of Filey Road and Seacliffe Road, using a high-lift Trevithick steam water pump. A hundred-foot well was sunk between Cayton and Osgodby in 1872 and its water was pumped to the Osgodby Top reservoir.

Seven years later, in a search for a new source of water supply, bore holes were drilled into the continuously wet fields near Irton, steam pumps installed, and water lifted to the reservoirs on the heights of Weaponess. Since then, the pumps have been converted from steam to electricity.

This impressive Victorian building, now the Eldin Hall Luxury Holiday Cottages, once housed the Cornish-style steam engines which pumped water from the aquifer under the Vale of Pickering to the reservoir at Osgodby Bank Top.

Water makes astonishing journeys. Some of the water at Irton comes from the River Derwent, which starts its journey ten miles away on Fylingdales Moor. When it reaches the weir in Forge Valley near East Ayton, it dives down a swallow hole in the river bed to arrive in the fields below the pumping station at Irton some six hours later. From Irton much of the water goes to the Springhill reservoir at the top of Falsgrave Park, a few yards from the source of Scarborough's water in medieval times!

Above In 1884 the Irton Water Works began to function. A fine piece of Victorian engineering, the building housed two large beam engine power pumps capable of producing 1,250,000 gallons of water a day from the 428-foot well to the reservoirs on top of Oliver's Mount.

Left Scarborough's water flows from Fylingdales Moor to Forge Valley where it dives down a 'swallow hole' in the river bed to the aquifer below the Vale of Pickering only to be lifted up again at the Irton Water Works into the reservoirs on Oliver's Mount, Falsgrave Park and Osgodby Top.

Trade in Scarborough

From its foundation in the twelfth century, Scarborough relied on trade for its very survival.

Early trading in a royal borough

The new royal borough of Scarborough was given its charter in about 1163. The town's inhabitants had no farmland and made their living principally by catching, preserving and selling fish. The sheriff at the Castle took some free fish for the king of England and bought many more at privileged low prices for the royal household. Great lords and monasteries sent their agents to buy fish. Some acquired an interest in houses for which rent was paid in herrings instead of money. Early craftsmen included carpenters, masons and a lime burner, mercers, tailors and girdlers, bakers, fish washers and flesh-hewers, coopers and rope-makers. Several metal trades flourished. Weavers organised an early craft guild and the borough enjoyed the rarely granted right to dye cloth. Salt was made on the sands. A few merchants exported wool and imported wine. Regular weekly trading was concentrated in a few streets near market crosses. The oldest market place was near St Mary's Church, which claimed a twentieth of each fisherman's catch as tithe and sold any surplus. Scarborough grew rapidly after 1253, when King Henry III granted its burgesses the right to hold a great forty-five day fish fair on the sands, the famous Scarborough Fair commemorated in song. When merchants from afar came to buy and distant mariners to fish the offshore waters, Scarborians dried or salted their fish and victualled their ships.

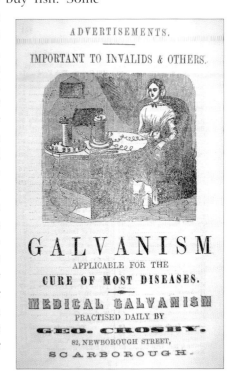

ADVERTISEMENTS.

IMPORTANT TO INVALIDS & OTHERS.

GALVANISM

APPLICABLE FOR THE

CURE OF MOST DISEASES.

MEDICAL GALVANISM

PRACTISED DAILY BY

GEO. CROSBY,

82, NEWBOROUGH STREET,

SCARBOROUGH.

Above Unusual services offered in Scarborough.

Scarborough Ware

Broken fragments of pottery turn up on every archaeological dig in Scarborough and tell us a great deal about the widespread trading links of the town. Scarborough was an important pottery-making centre in the Middle Ages. The kilns were situated along Castle Road, just within the Old Borough defences, where the natural glacial clay was particularly suitable for making pots. The pottery was used extensively in the town and by most of the local villages but was also traded abroad through the port. The distinctive Scarborough Ware has been discovered at archaeological excavations in Scandinavia and the Low Countries and pieces have even turned up in Iceland! Jugs

Opposite One of the famous 'Scarborough' novelties.

A Scarborough Ware water jug or aquamanile found on the site of the potteries. It is covered in a lustrous green glaze and has been modelled in the form of a ram with applied pellets of clay representing wool. The potters of medieval Scarborough were clearly very skilful craftsmen.

made at the Scarborough kilns were often covered in a bright green glaze and adorned with human faces or the figures of armoured knights. Other vessels for carrying water, called aquamaniles, were modelled to look like animals and must have been highly prized tableware. After the Scarborough pottery industry ended in the fourteenth century, the townsfolk had to buy their earthenware from potteries in Ryedale and around the Humber basin. Much was imported across the North Sea, from the Low Countries and Germany. Even pottery made in Spain 500 years ago has been found by archaeologists digging in the Old Town.

A dual revival: Port and resort

New prosperity came to Scarborough in the seventeenth century. As more coal was exported from the Northumberland and Durham fields, Scarborough became an important port, supplying ships that carried the coal and acting as a haven of refuge for colliers moving down the coast. A levy on the coal trade saved the harbour from decay. A major shipbuilding industry spread along the harbour side. Scarborough built and worked many colliers and other vessels in the growing Baltic and Russia trades. Scandinavian deal timber, tow and tar were imported, as well as flax for local linen cloth and sail-making. Butter and linen cloth became major exports.

The same century saw wealthy Spa visitors requiring exotic luxury goods. As the resort grew in the eighteenth century, there were specialised shops just for visitors. William Lease made and sold clocks. Sedan chair men, fancy cooks and an upholsterer came from London. Peruke makers sold wigs and grocers opened shops. Nanny

Salmon at first sold pebbles from the beach, but later her stall became a fancy goods warehouse. Everything appeared that the richest in the kingdom might require. They could buy dogs, patent medicines, lottery tickets, books from Fleet Street or the *York Courant* newspaper. Deards opened a toy shop. Dalrymple the cotton promoter and Thompson the Nottingham hosier held low-price ex-factory sales at the Long Rooms. In one trip alone, a visitor named Sitwell spent 31 guineas at Scarborough and York shops, buying Indian stuffs, velvet, tea, coffee and handkerchiefs. The visitors' town moved uphill to the new shopping centre at Newborough, Queen Street and St Nicholas Street.

A greater trade

Scarborough saw almost every known type of shop after 1845, when the railway brought more visitors and a growing volume of goods made elsewhere. Many were mass produced but small workshops often remained behind Scarborough's retail shops. Greensmith & Thackwray in St Nicholas Street were hosiers with royal patronage. They began by selling Irish point lace and Balbriggan stockings, but grew to supply braces, Burberry waterproofs and sea-bathing towels. Big ironmongers and furnishing stores serviced the lodging houses. Francis Haigh's cabinet-making workshop late in the century became Tonks' upholsterers, with great plate glass windows illuminating four floors. Several shops expanded to new large sites in Westborough as the centre for shopping moved further west towards the railway station. William Rowntree's house furnishers became a department store, where ten bays of great windows held 200 incandescent lamps and employees enjoyed profit sharing. At one extreme, Coulson was court hairdresser to the Duke and Duchess of Teck; at the other, William Boyes pioneered the Remnant Warehouse, filling 600 feet of counters with factory remnants and much else. 'None were pressed to buy.' If you couldn't afford a new hat, you could afford a ribbon at Boyes to brighten up an old one. His publication, the *Remnant Warehouse Messenger*, advertised everything from dolls' houses at six shillings to pop guns and rubber bubbles. During the same shopping boom, wholesalers sought any outlet, so every Scarborough street corner gained a general store. For the 'respectable and necessitous poor', there were the winter soup kitchens with soup at a penny a quart.

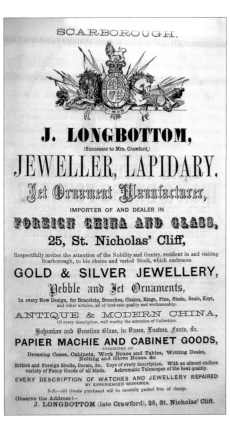

The birth of 'fancy goods' in Scarborough.

Above Washing machines for Scarborough's landladies.

Below The new Scarborough linoleum made for boarding house floors.

Manufacture

Local manufacturers supplied the resort's demands. Brewing changed from a situation where each alehouse brewed its own to three breweries. One of these was Godfrey Knight's, rebuilt at North Street in 1850, which became the Scarborough and Whitby Brewery Company with seventy tied public houses. Enoch Tindall's foundry supplied everything in iron, from washing machines to kitchen ranges and second-floor verandas. Samuel Hawksworth's Patent Tile Floor Company laid thick paint layers on canvas to make a durable, waterproof sanitary flooring. In brick works on Seamer Road the steam presses made 8,000 bricks a day and steam-heated sheds dried 40,000 to 50,000 bricks a week to feed the building boom which took Scarborough north, west and south over the old field landscape. By the close of Queen Victoria's reign, 174 cab and carriage owners moved visitors around and there were several great livery stables. When the postage on cards was reduced and writing allowed on the back, E.T. Dennis pioneered picture postcards. Special Scarborough items enjoyed a brief fame. E. Jackson of the Medical Hall at 20 Newborough sold the

In 1852 an extensive area occupied by butchers' shops, slaughterhouses and tallow and bone yards, known as the Old Shambles, was cleared to make way for the new public Market Hall which opened the following year. Designed by John Irvin, borough surveyor, in the Tuscan style with a Whitby stone facade, it is considered one of the most handsome buildings in Scarborough. Alluding to the town's long history of market trading, two roundels on the building's frontage depict the borough seal which includes a form of medieval trading vessel known as a cog.

perfume 'Scarborough Bouquet' and John Gibson, the Admiralty optician, the 'Scarborough' telescope. Hopper and Mason's great store sold the 'Scarborough Skirt of fearnought serge which would neither shrink nor spot'. Mrs. Taylor's royal butterscotch and simmel cakes were sampled by the Prince of Wales in 1871, so the royal face was moulded onto the side of her pork pies. During the so-called naughty nineties the town gave its name to a sober garment, 'the Scarborough', really a loose-fitting sleeveless overcoat with deep armholes and an elbow-length cape.

Street selling

Street selling continued on market days. Poultry, butter and eggs could be purchased in St Nicholas Street, hardware and pots in St Thomas Street, 'all sorts' at about eighty Newborough stalls, and drapery and hats in Queen Street. The great new Market Hall of 1853 replaced much of this outdoor trade by a rich assemblage of stalls and shops under cover. The Sandside cockle and whelk stalls visited by Anne Brontë remained, but the Victorian Scarborough Corporation sought to limit much street selling, not altogether successfully. An 1891 visitor was impressed by street musicians en masse, hurdy gurdy players and organ grinders, photographers, apple girls, hirers of drawers and towels, and sellers of elastic balls. Famed street calls included Bland crying 'cockles alive o' and Mrs Hick's high soprano 'any fish today'. Billie Donkin cried 'pies, all hot'. An Italian ice-cream seller on the sands shouted 'hokey pokey penny a lump, that's the stuff that makes you jump.'

Even today, stalls on Sandside sell fresh shellfish, doughnuts, ice cream and candy floss all year round to visitors. You may also hear the Town Crier announce a bargain in Scarborough's streets.

DICKY DICKINSON,
Governour of Scarborough Spaw.

SAMOS unenvy'd boasts her Æsop gone,
And FRANCE may glory in her late Scarron,
While ENGLAND has a Living Dickinson.

Sold by C. Ward & R. Chandler near Temple Barr, & at their shop in Scarborough.

The first seaside resort

The discovery of mineral springs under the South Bay cliff at Scarborough in about 1626 attracted visitors seeking the benefits of its spa waters. The town adapted itself over the years to meet their needs.

Spa water – of inky smell and acid taste – to drink

The books of Dr Robert Wittie of York promoted the waters of Scarborough Spa as a cure for 'melancholic vapours, nightmares, apoplexy, catalepsie, epilepsie, vertigo, nerves, yellow and black jaundice'. Soon, the healthy followed the sick, for the 'nimbly purging' waters offered them equal benefits. By 1667, 'people of good fashion' were coming to Scarborough. On their first day in town, the sick and the healthy consulted doctors, who advised a stay of four to five weeks, between mid-May and mid-September, with daily drinking of five to eight pints of spa water. Two half-pints consumed early in the morning were followed by exercise on the sands and this pattern was continued until dinner time.

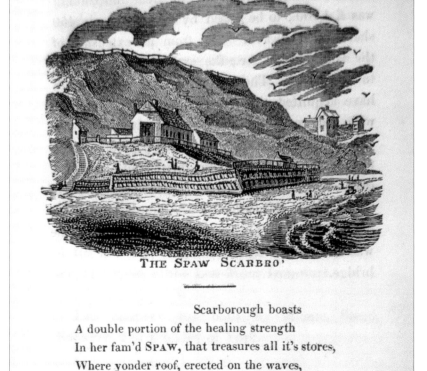

THE SPAW SCARBRO'

Scarborough boasts
A double portion of the healing strength
In her fam'd SPAW, that treasures all it's stores,
Where yonder roof, erected on the waves,
Grotesquely lurks beneath the pendent cliff.

FOSTER.

Opposite Dicky Dickinson was appointed Spa governor in 1698. Much mocked for his unusual appearance, he gave as good as he got and was remembered for his wit and impudence. By keeping a wine cellar and selling newspapers, he became better off than some who mocked him. His face was often carved on walking sticks.

Behold the governor of Scarborough spaw, the strangest phiz and form you ever saw

Yet, when you view the beauties of his mind, in him a second Aesop you may find

Left The first Spa structure was a simple platform of rocks bound by timbers near the springs which received twice-daily inundations from the tide. The Spa governor lived in the house behind. He collected subscriptions, sold newspapers and supervised more than eight widows, who used cups on long wands to dip the water and drinking horns to serve it. The first governor built 'rooms of convenience', with leaves deposited at the entry. The Duchess of Marlborough was so appalled at the communal 'ladies assembly' that she had bottled Spa water delivered to her lodging.

The great discovery: Nature's playground of sand and sea

Scarborough was the first spa resort by the sea. The old Bath, Buxton, Tunbridge and Epsom spas and the new northern spa at Knaresborough–Harrogate were all inland. The 'innocent recreations' of the sandy sea beach were novelties which made all the difference between Scarborough and the rest. Some visitors, such as the naturalist John Ray, wandered the sands picking up gemstones. Others raced on horse or foot.

View all the scenes the world around,
There's none like Scarbro can be found

Doctor Wittie had urged sea bathing for gout but sea bathing for fun soon became all the rage. No one objected when some London doctors became convinced that cold water bathing was itself healthy and could produce cures. Inland spas such as Epsom installed small baths but it was not the same.

Let Epsom, Tunbridge, Knaresborough be
In what request they will, Scarborough for me

A. The Spaw House   B. Mill Beck   C. The Long Room   D. Blands Cliff Road   To the Hon.ble JOHN HILL E.s.
West Sand Gate   F. The Post House   G. East Sand Gate   H. The Town Hall   This PERSPECTIVE Draught of the ANT

In 1662 Sir John Reresby noticed that 'many persons of quality came that Summer for their health or their diversion'; Dr Simpson soon observed that some came 'just for the diversion'.

Noble visitors

Over 1,000 visitors were recorded at Scarborough in 1733, including earls and knights galore. In later seasons visitors declined to around 500 people, but when the Duke of York came for the first of three visits in 1761 there was a fashionable revival. On the first day, he opened the ball at the Long Room (part ballroom and part casino) with Lady Caroline Montagu, and then played cards. The northern aristocracy was well represented. The Duke of Rutland is credited with making the town the 'gay assembly of the north' and his son, the Marquess of Granby and a popular army commander, visited annually until his death. During one summer it was said that there was no news in London because everyone was at Scarborough.

John Setterington's print of 1725 shows the spa buildings and visitors on the nearby sands. By 1733 it was the custom for 'not only the gentlemen but the ladies also to bathe in the sea. The men went out a short distance in boats and jumped in the water naked. The ladies had two small dressing rooms, gowns and guides to lead them to the water.' The new seeing glasses were used to watch the collier fleets go by, or catch 'nymphs emerging from the sea'. The beach was a ready-made carriage drive, a promenade on which to see and be seen: 'There, no distinction is made of quality but high and low equally privileged, pass and repass, mix and separate, as it were in the Elysian fields.'

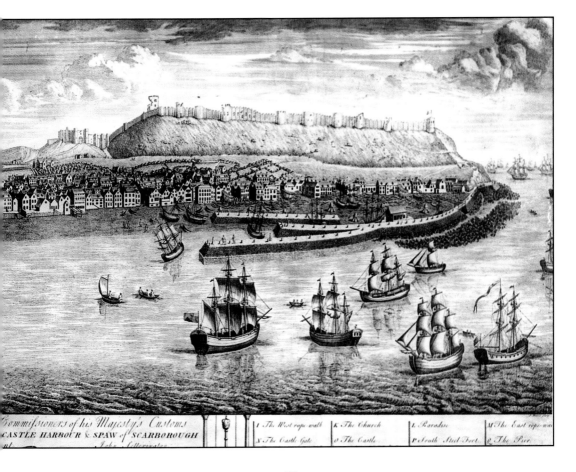

Commissioners of his Majesty's Customs
CASTLE HARBOUR & SPAW of SCARBOROUGH

| I The West rope walk | K The Church | L Paradise | M The East rope wa |
| N The Castle Gate | O The Castle | P South Steel Fort | Q The Pier |

The move to the upper town

Public breakfasts en déshabille at eleven in the morning became fashionable, with music followed by dancing until two o'clock when dinner began. Scarborough fish were a visitor's treat. A dried and salted large fish like a cod was dressed, watered, wired, roasted at the fire, and served with a good sauce. Lodging-house keepers provided food at 'ordinaries', where 'persons of all ranks sat down together' and dined on ten or twelve dishes. Inns sent meals to lodgings or visitors could dine at the coffee house, long rooms or Spa house.

Early diversions were largely confined to the sands but the growing company of 'spawers' demanded sociable, indoor pastimes for the rest of the day.

> Cock fighting they'd discuss, then baiting too
> Or dicing at a Scarborough inn or two,
> With wit and wisdom passed from man to man
> Down from the palaces of good Queen Anne

Old taverns and inns, many early lodging houses and the first three 'long rooms' were in lower Scarborough, now referred to as the Old Town. By 1733, a large new assembly room had been built for dancing and gambling at the bottom of St Nicholas Street which, with Newborough Street and Queen Street, formed the new fashionable quarter referred to as the upper town. From this time onward, the lower town was ignored and left to the shipbuilders and mariners who lived there. The Spa and the sands were for the morning and the upper town was for the afternoon and evening. The upper town was given paved roads and flagged walkways. Here were the new Queen Street horse fair, Ward's book shop and circulating library, and the dog kennels which housed the Scarborough Corporation's pack of hounds. Here also were the new bowling greens, a coffee house, billiard rooms and Kerragan's afternoon booth theatre near the Crown and Sceptre, replaced in 1767 by evening performances at the Playhouse in St Thomas Street. In about 1787, William Bean opened a public garden in which visitors could promenade, just outside Newborough near what is now Huntriss Row.

A quieter resort

New sea bathing resorts at Brighton, Deal, Eastbourne, Southsea and Exmouth were spreading the aristocracy more thinly around the country. By 1730 Scarborough was beginning to welcome the newly prosperous middle classes from the commercial counties. Ever more visitors came by horse, private carriage and the new steamboats. Wilberforce, Captain Bligh, Arkwright of Derby, Madame Tussaud, Lord Byron (smitten with a Quaker lass), Sir Robert Peel and country squires all came, but so did parsons, shopkeepers and school masters in coaches from Nottingham, Hull, Leeds and Newcastle. This new class of visitor was less racy and more respectable than the old aristocracy. Scarborough responded with more serious attractions: a subscription news room, circulating libraries and museums to display collected fossils and specimens. The coffee house was converted to a bookshop and the assembly rooms restricted gambling and dancing. Artists and musicians gave lessons. Three 'camera obscura' were erected for panoramic viewing.

The first visitor accommodations were in the houses of gentlemen, merchants and mariners. Many houses were rebuilt in the eighteenth century for dual use by wealthy visitors in summer and owners in winter. Soon, lodging houses were purpose built for letting. The 'new buildings' of the 1760s had sash windows in brick walls, deal floors, neat pedimented doorways and many chambers. A sea view became desirable. South of the borough ditch on the cliff was St Nicholas Cliff, shown below, which by 1770 had gained several 'superior lodging houses' around a railed promenade garden.

Right Not everyone enjoyed sea bathing. Healthy plungers into the cold sea were warned that

When the bathing does not produce a moderate glow after quitting the water, When the chilling sensation continues, When the extremities become cold, the spirits lanquid, the head disordered or the appetite impaired ...

and advised to reconsider.

Five new indoor baths with pumped and warmed sea water, such as the one shown here, must have seemed a welcome alternative.

Below Shopping became a new indulgence. Bland's mercery, Deard's toy shop and a Nottingham hosier exhibiting silk pieces for waistcoats in the Long Room gave way to London shops opening branches for the season. Marshall & Snellgrove opened a permanent branch in 1838. New bazaars invited visitors to 'lounge'. James Schofield in his contemporary guidebook mocked the new fancy goods shops offering 'knick knacks of life of little value to anyone but their vendor' but they clearly had a future! Cracknells on Cliff Terrace displayed fancy goods in the new double bow windows which were replacing the older Georgian shop fronts.

A place to stay

A furnished house in 1803 could be let for six to ten guineas, and there were apartments as well. The new 'board and lodging houses' took hold slowly. The new 'hotel' sought to provide everything for the rich, who found it hardly necessary to venture outside. Donner's Hotel, which took over the Long Room in 1815, could seat 210 for dinner and was probably the first hotel in the north of England. Dr Granville saw this, the forerunner of today's Royal Hotel, as the best hotel of its class in the 'Queen of English sea-bathing places', with vistas which he likened to the Bay of Naples. His only complaint was that visitors did not return a bow and only danced with one of their own set.

The coming of the railway in 1845 transformed Scarborough from spa to holiday resort. One excursion train arriving at its station could deposit more visitors than the town had in earlier times welcomed in an entire season.

The Crown Hotel, built along the new Esplanade on the South Cliff in 1843, pioneered a suite system, which offered privacy in a group of rooms including sitting room, bedroom and dressing room, as well as first-class public rooms, and was supported by numerous stables and carriage stands.

SCARBOROUGH OPEN AIR THEATRE

SEASON 1938 : JULY 25th to SEPT. 12th

PAGEANT OF TANNHÄUSER

Performances : Mondays & Thursdays.   Seating for 6,000 Spectators.

The later resort

The coming of the railways and improvements to the town's water supply led to a period of great growth and development for Scarborough, 'the Queen of Watering Places'.

Victorian and Edwardian holiday resort

The York to Scarborough railway, opened in 1845, was followed two years later by the Scarborough to Bridlington branch and a direct service to Hull. Later lines were opened to Pickering and to Whitby. The town prospered as people found it easier to travel to the coast, the fashion for day trips began and new types of visitor started to arrive.

The town grew, with the South Cliff developing rapidly after the opening of the Valley Bridge in 1865. The construction of Eastborough enabled easier access to the South Bay, where the Foreshore Road between the harbour and the Spa Bridge was constructed in 1877. The Royal Albert Drive alongside the North Bay, opened in 1890, was followed by the Marine Drive linking the two bays, a tremendous engineering feat, which was opened in 1908. Now it was possible for visitors to stroll for miles by the sea, walking from the quiet and relatively undeveloped North Bay to the bustling harbour area and the attractions of the South Bay.

Opposite Railway company posters were often very striking visually, as in this 1938 example of cooperation between the LNER and Scarborough Council. Both organisations were anxious to attract more visitors to the resort.

Below The pier was the main tourist attraction in the relatively undeveloped North Bay. Never a great success financially, in spite of various improvements during its short history, it was destroyed by a gale in 1905.

A variety of types and quality of accommodation was to be found in the town. The Crown Hotel was the pre-eminent hotel until the opening of the Grand in 1867, the largest hotel in Europe at the time. Near the station was the Pavilion Hotel, on the South Cliff the Prince of Wales and on the North Cliff the Alexandra and the Queen's hotels.

The Spa, the Grand Hotel and the Foreshore Road all appear in this 1892 view of the late Victorian resort, which had developed greatly as the railways brought more and more visitors to the town.

Various temperance hotels existed, including Thornham's and Thomas Whittaker's. There were also boarding houses such as Swift's.

Transport facilities improved. Cliff lifts, of which Scarborough was to have more than any other British resort, helped visitors cope with the town's hilly terrain. The first, the South Cliff Tramway near the Spa, opened in 1875. Four years later the Scarborough Omnibus Company began to operate horse-buses from Castle Road to Falsgrave and from the North Cliff to the Esplanade on the South Cliff. Finally, in 1904, long after many other resorts had introduced them, trams arrived in the town. These ran to the West Pier, the Spa, the Floral Hall and Falsgrave.

Sea bathing remained very popular with the visitors and was now done largely for pleasure rather than for health. Bathing machines were a highly visible feature on the sands of both bays. The Victorians regulated bathing, trying to ensure that those who went in the sea were decently attired and that the sexes were segregated.

For better-off visitors, the Spa was still the centre of the town's social life and it kept expanding to meet demand; its pavilion was enlarged in 1847 and again in 1858. After a disastrous fire in 1876, a new Spa was built which became known for the high standard of its music. The Spa flourished as the town's major attraction until the outbreak of the Second World War.

Other attractions of the resort included sea trips, visits to the nearby countryside and walks in the town's many gardens. The Holbeck, Clarence, St. Nicholas, Belvedere and Alexandra Gardens were opened in the decades before 1914; Peasholm Park was developed and the People's Park became the Valley Gardens. Holidaymakers could visit the Aquarium, opened in 1877, or Catlin's New Arcadia (1909) or watch the pierrots on the sands. They could visit the Rotunda Museum, expanded in the 1860s. In the evenings they could patronise the Theatre Royal or the Prince of Wales Circus, both in St Thomas Street, or the Londesborough Theatre in Westborough. Before the First World War the town's first picture house had opened, as had the Floral Hall on the North Side. Scarborough's entertainments, like its accommodation, catered for a range of visitors from different social classes.

The South Bay Pool, opened in 1915, was a great success and was copied by other resorts. It was one of the town's major attractions in the inter-war period and is seen here on a postcard sent in 1930. The pool was developed further in the 1930s. Closed in the 1980s, it has now been filled in.

Inter-war developments

Scarborough Council was increasingly aware of the need for good publicity and the town began to advertise itself more effectively through its guides for visitors.

Early attempts to attract visitors to the North Side, such as the Rock Gardens of 1860 and the North Bay Pier of 1869, had not been great successes; the facilities had anticipated a demand that was not really there. Now, however, the time was ripe and the development of the North Side was the most prominent feature of the inter-war years, aided by the construction of Northway which linked Westborough and Columbus Ravine and helped to open up the area.

Peasholm Park was extended and improved with the addition of Peasholm Glen and the introduction of the naval battles on the lake. The Corner Café was opened in 1925, the North Bay Promenade was extended northwards and a cliff lift was constructed at Peasholm Gap, the entrance to the North Bay, in 1930.

Very important developments occurred in the area that became known as Northstead Manor Gardens. In 1931 the miniature railway was opened. It attracted so many passengers that a second locomotive was added in the following year and, in spite of a fatal accident in 1932, it proved a good revenue-earner for Scarborough Corporation. So also did the Open Air Theatre, the first production at which was Sir Edward German's light opera *Merrie England* in 1932. Situated in a natural amphitheatre and with seating for over 7,000 people, it was very popular. Local amateurs, members of the Scarborough Amateur Operatic and Dramatic Society, were the mainstays of the productions, which were renowned for spectacular sets, costumes and effects.

After a short life the motor boat pool in Peasholm Gap, derided by residents as 'the Puny Pool', was replaced in 1938 by the North Bay Bathing Pool. It still exists, though now as a fun pool, Atlantis.

Still a firm favourite today, the North Bay Railway was opened in 1931, running from Peasholm to a station near the beach and then to Scalby Mills. Its first locomotives, named Triton and Neptune, were exact scale models of the LNER's Gresley engines, but were diesel powered rather than driven by steam.

The North Side witnessed the building of many smaller hotels in the Northstead area as this part of Scarborough became more frequented by visitors, aided by the increased bus services which replaced the trams in the 1930s. Holiday camps and caravan parks also grew in popularity as Scarborough catered for a wider and wider range of holidaymakers. The authors of the Adshead Report, a town-planning investigation, commented in 1938 that the town was 'better able to entertain all classes than any other seaside resort in England'.

The South Bay still attracted many visitors. This was the heyday of the South Bay Pool as it, and the beach, attracted not only bathers but also many devotees of the new sunbathing craze. The Spa was still a major entertainment centre and there were more and more establishments on the Foreshore where visitors could amuse themselves. American influences were apparent in the soda fountains at the Spa and in the Futurist cinema, one of many in the town.

Visitors also found a great variety of sporting opportunities. Cricket, golf and tennis festivals and tournaments were well attended, as were swimming championships and motor sport events, though the proposal to make Scarborough the centre of British motor racing by constructing a ten-mile circuit on Seamer and Irton Moors came to nothing.

A holidaymaker wrote in 1938:

> *Having a fine time here. Met a nice bit of Huddersfield but*
> *she went back yesterday. Saw the Amateur Championship*
> *1 Mile + Plain Dive this morning, Tennis Championships on this*
> *week. Will be dancing to Lou Preager at the Spa tonight.*
> *(To lofty heights my spirit mounts,*
> *For a week, I'm rid of those d_____d accounts.)*

As some new developments prospered, other old favourites, such as the Theatre Royal, disappeared or were changed; for example, the

Aquarium became Gala Land, an underground funfair. The town pondered its future. The existence of divisions and rivalries, for example between South Cliff and North Bay and between advocates of private enterprise and supporters of municipal provision, suggests that there was already some concern about the continuing prosperity of the town. To attract visitors cost the town money; some wanted to concentrate on keeping the rates down in order to attract more permanent residents.

Decline and rejuvenation in the resort

Different types of accommodation developed. In 1971 Scarborough still had 365 hotels, but already some were being converted to meet the demand for self-catering flats. A number of important holiday camps and caravan sites on the outskirts of the town bore witness to another new trend. With the growth of foreign holidays and short breaks in Britain, the provision of bed and breakfast accommodation increased.

Some old attractions closed, including many of the town's cinemas, the Floral Hall, the South Bay Pool and the Open Air Theatre. Bingo halls became more popular. In the same period Peasholm Park continued to be developed, with the illuminated tree walk opening in 1953.

The railways experienced a period of contraction, with the Seamer–Pickering and Scarborough–Whitby lines closing, as more and more visitors arrived by car, in spite of the poor access roads.

Nevertheless, some attractions, such as Kinderland, have prospered and new facilities have been developed, including the indoor swimming pool and the Stephen Joseph Theatre. In the early years of the new century the Marine Drive is being strengthened and there are proposals for a major development on the North Side.

Shows were staged at the Open Air Theatre, 'this Drury Lane of the open air', as it was described by one contemporary writer, from the 1930s to the 1960s. The operas of the 1930s were followed by musicals after the Second World War.

Although no longer as reliant on holidaymakers as it was, the town still has a future as a major resort.

The Rotunda Museum was initially built to house the collection of the Scarborough historian Thomas Hinderwell. The pioneering geologist William Smith (1769–1839) suggested a circular design as best suited to displaying specimens, and a York man, Richard Hey Sharp (1793–1853), was architect. The Rotunda Museum was opened in 1828 and two wings were added in 1861.

Culture and the arts in Scarborough

Culture and the arts in Scarborough developed largely, though not exclusively, for the entertainment and recreation of summer visitors.

Stage and screen

As early as 1734 visitors to Scarborough were being entertained by Mr Kerragan's company of actors, brought from York for the summer season.

The opening of the railway in 1845 brought more visitors from all social classes demanding different forms of entertainment. Holding 2,500, the Prince of Wales Circus in St Thomas Street hosted Adam's Circus, gymnastic and equestrian displays, concerts and lectures. Later known as Zalva's Hippodrome, in 1908 it was redeveloped as a conventional theatre and became known as the Opera House.

When Scarborough Spa was rebuilt in 1879 after a major fire, a theatre was included in the new building where summer shows and Christmas pantomimes are still produced. There were also outdoor theatres: Pierrots performed on elaborate stages set up on the beach and in 1932 Scarborough's Open Air Theatre was opened in Northstead Manor Gardens with the stage on an island in the lake.

In the late 1700s, wealthy visitors whiled away the afternoon at the theatre on Tanner Street (now St Thomas Street), where many famous actors performed. In 1825 a seat in the boxes cost three shillings, in the pit two shillings and in the gallery one shilling. The theatre was demolished in 1924.

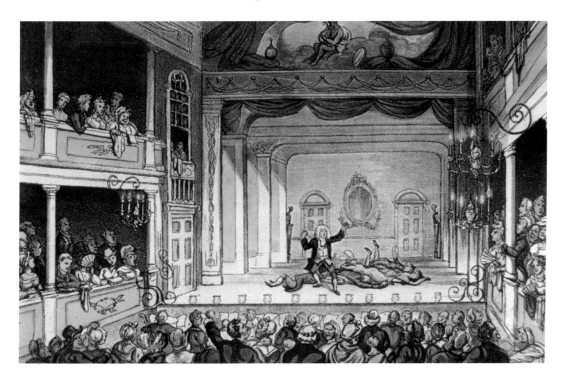

Moving films began life in Scarborough as a curiosity and were shown in any suitable hall or theatre. Soon, purpose-built cinemas appeared such as the North Bay Picture House (now the Hollywood Plaza) (1914), the Palladium Picture House (1914), the Aberdeen Walk Picture House (1920), the Futurist (1921) and the Capitol (1929). The Odeon (1936) was part of Oscar Deutsch's nation-wide chain and now houses the Stephen Joseph Theatre where Scarborough playwright, Sir Alan Ayckbourn, premieres his new work. Though much altered internally, it is nonetheless one of the few remaining Odeon cinemas in the country, and the outside has been carefully restored to its original appearance. It houses both the Theatre in the Round and the McCarthy Theatre, a studio theatre where films are also shown.

Books, guides and newspapers

From Scarborough's earliest days as a resort, seasonal visitors could keep up with their reading by joining subscription libraries stocked with the latest books. In 1787 the library at James Schofield's bookshop boasted 4,000 volumes ranging from 'light summer reading ... to more serious works of learned and elegant writers'. Subscriptions were expensive – from five shillings to half a guinea, the latter allowing the borrower six books at a time.

In 1848, George Beeforth's New Book, Print & Music Establishment, Public Library & Newsroom promised 'most of the popular books of the day including the works of Scott, Bulwer, James, Cooper, Dickens, Mrs Gore, Mrs Trollope, Lady Blessington etc. . . . and new works and magazines will constantly be added.' From as early as

Besides providing subscription libraries, bookshops were also popular meeting places for the summer visitors. Note the fashionable black servant in this print of a Scarborough bookshop in 1812.

1732, local guidebooks were being published, many by Scarborough bookshop owners.

Newspapers – national, county and local – were provided by the bookshops. The Scarborough papers published weekly lists of visitors for the socially conscious gentry to consult.

Learned societies, the Mechanics' Institute and a literary family

Several private museums were established in the town to display the rich assortment of fossils and minerals found along the coast. Mr Hornsey of King Street, a schoolmaster and drawing teacher, opened his natural history museum to the public in the early 1800s.

The Scarborough Philosophical Society was founded in 1827 and built the Rotunda as its permanent museum. Later, a group interested in the 'gentlemanly' excavation of prehistoric burial mounds on local estates founded the Archaeological Society. It amalgamated with the Philosophical Society in 1853.

In 1851 the Mechanics' Institute took over the Odd Fellows Hall (now Scarborough Library) in Vernon Place, where evening classes were held for 'reading, writing, arithmetic, drawing and modelling'.

Originally, learned societies were for the upper classes but in 1830 a Mechanics' Institute was founded in Scarborough by Mr J. B. Baker with the aim of educating skilled craftsmen. Its premises in Long Room Street (now St Nicholas Street) included a library, and lectures on such subjects as mineralogy, electricity and antiquities were delivered to 'crowded audiences'.

Wood End in The Crescent, which today houses the Natural History Museum, was bought in 1870 by Lady Louisa Sitwell as a seaside home for her family, a change from their main residence at Renishaw Hall, Derbyshire. Lady Louisa gave Wood End to her son George in 1886 and his family continued to use it as a second home until the 1920s. He married 'the girl next door', the daughter of their neighbour in The Crescent, Lord Londesborough of Londesborough Lodge.

Sir George Sitwell's eldest child, the poet Edith Sitwell (1887–1964), born in Scarborough, is particularly remembered for *Façade*, an entertainment in which she read her own words to music by Sir William Walton. The second child Osbert (1892–1969), wrote a five-volume autobiography, *Left Hand, Right Hand!*, which included an account of his life in Scarborough where he stood for Parliament as Liberal candidate in 1919. The youngest child, Sacheverell (1897–1988), wrote about his experiences as a traveller as well as poetry and articles on art and architecture.

Prints, landscape paintings and art galleries

Guidebooks were not illustrated until the early 1800s when woodcuts or engravings of local scenes from drawings and paintings by Scarborough artists such as Mathew Baynes (1793–1866) began to

be included. The bookshops sold prints of local views taken from paintings by local and visiting landscape and marine artists.

Victorian businessmen set up art galleries in Scarborough to exhibit nationally famous paintings and to display and sell the work of local artists. Many professional painters from Britain and Europe were attracted to Scarborough, hoping to find a ready market for their paintings. John Atkinson Grimshaw (1836–1893) was a highly successful self-taught artist from Leeds whose Scarborough home was Castle by the Sea in Mulgrave Place.

Above Henry Barlow Carter (1804–1868) had a successful career in Scarborough much assisted by his association with Solomon Wilkinson Theakston, bookshop owner and proprietor of the *Scarborough Gazette*. Carter's drawings were used to illustrate both the *Gazette* and *Theakston's Guides*, and his original paintings were displayed and sold in Theakston's shop.

Portraits, silhouettes and photographs

Portrait painters frequented Scarborough in the season from the mid-1700s. At the beginning of the 1840s Mr Lowther charged one guinea for a miniature portrait but cheaper alternatives were offered by silhouettists. Mr Sherwood, from London and Brighton, produced 'a correct profile likeness with the scissors from one shilling'. The Irish silhouettist Patrick Wybrant offered a 'strictly correct likeness' at his Likeness Gallery at 1 Newborough Street, with prices from one shilling and sixpence to twenty-one shillings. His advertising handbill grimly reminded his potential clients that 'a good likeness is all we can rescue from the grave.'

Dancing and music

Dancing at grand balls was a popular but formal evening pastime in Scarborough.

Scarborough has a long musical tradition, both amateur and professional. Thus, visitors in 1825 could take music lessons from Mr Hartley or hire a piano for the season from one of five dealers. Musical entertainment at the Spa began in Henry Wyatt's Gothic saloon of 1839

Right Oliver Sarony (1820–79), a Canadian entrepreneur, set up a grand studio in Scarborough where he made portraits painted on an enlarged photographic base into luxury products. At its height Sarony's Studio was said to be the largest in Europe.

and, when Joseph Paxton extended the buildings in 1857, both a music hall and a bandstand were central features of his design.

Brass bands have always been popular, particularly in contests – although one in July 1859 probably took second place to a balloon ascent, organised on the same day by a Scarborough man, Mr Lundy. In the later nineteenth century Scarborough Sundays were alive with the sound of music with concerts at the Spa, the Aquarium, the North Bay Promenade Pier and the Old Town Hall.

A wide range of arts thrives in Scarborough today, while the Scarborough Archaeological and Historical Society, like its nineteenth-century predecessor, takes a lively interest in the town's past.

Above A 1787 guidebook informs visitors that the proprietors of the two assembly rooms on Long Room Street (now St Nicholas Street), William Newstead and Edward Donner, had both agreed to organise one 'dress' ball and two 'undress' balls each week. A subscription to each of the rooms cost half a guinea. A further payment of half a guinea allowed entrance to all 'dress' balls for the season although no further charge was made for 'undress' balls. However, '... gentlemen who dance country dances pay 2 shillings for music.'

Left Pritchard's Band (1867-1879) played at the Spa in the mid-Victorian era. When the Spa was rebuilt in 1879 after a major fire, the Grand Hall concert auditorium was, and still is, one of the central attractions of the tourist season. A permanent municipal orchestra, the Scarborough Spa Orchestra, was established and has had many notable musical directors including Max Jaffa. To this day it continues to entertain summer visitors as the longest surviving seaside orchestra.

Three walks in Scarborough

1. The Old Town

Before beginning this walk, try to view the model of medieval Scarborough on the first floor of the Natural History Museum at **Wood End** in The Crescent.

Begin on St. Nicholas Cliff outside the Grand Hotel, an area containing the long-vanished leper hospital of St. Nicholas that was outside the town walls. Cross Harcourt Place and walk along Bar Street, just inside the line of the medieval ditch, to Newborough, where a clock bearing the borough's seal marks the position of **Newborough Bar**, the main entrance to the town. Walk down Newborough until you reach St. Thomas Street, turn left and walk to its end, where the remaining fragment of the **medieval wall** can be seen in the YMCA car park. Proceed uphill on Castle Road to **St. Mary's Church** and the **Castle**. The platform inside the **Castle** gives an excellent view of the town and its setting.

From **St. Mary's Church** head down the steps to Church Stairs Street, passing the site of a chapel where John Wesley preached between 1759 and 1790. When you reach Longwestgate look right and left to get a good impression of

the grid layout of the medieval town. Then walk down St Mary's Street to Princess Square, where the Low Conduit was located, to see the remains of the medieval **Butter Cross** before proceeding up St. Sepulchre Street past **Trinity House** to the **Market Hall**. You are now in the area of the medieval **Old Borough** defences.

Next walk the few steps to Eastborough and cross it to see the fine eighteenth-century house at **37-39 Merchants Row** before following Eastborough towards the foreshore. Just before its bottom end, turn left into **The Bolts** and walk along this reminder of the medieval town until you get to **Quay Street**, where the house at **number 2** and the **Three Mariners** are rare examples of late medieval timber-framed buildings.

At the end of Quay Street, cross Sandside and walk out along the **Lighthouse Pier**, from which fine views of the town and the South Bay can be obtained. Then retrace your steps to Sandside, and walk along by the harbour and the beach to St. Nicholas Gardens. From here you can walk back up to St. Nicholas Cliff or get the cliff lift.

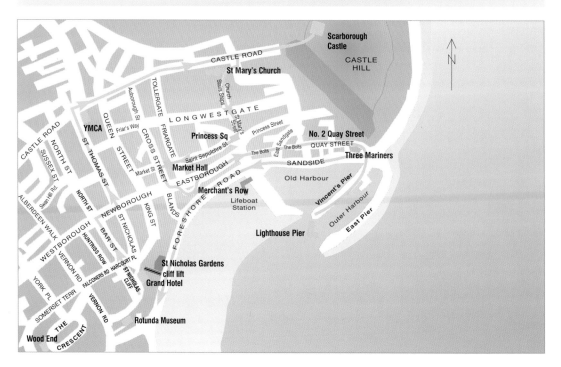

2. South Bay

Start on St Nicholas Cliff in front of the **Grand Hotel**, the largest in Europe when it was built in the 1860s. Cross the **Spa Bridge** and look to the right to see the **Rotunda Museum**. Climb up to the Esplanade and look at the buildings, particularly the **Crown Hotel**. Then walk along the Esplanade and admire the view of the South Bay before either taking the **cliff lift**, the first in Europe, down to the **Spa** or walking down to sea level via the **Italian** and **Rose Gardens**. Spend some time at the **Spa** studying its architecture, a mixture of different styles, before walking along Foreshore Road to the harbour area. Cross the road and walk back on the other side, which is full of modern amusement arcades and cafés. Walk through **St Nicholas Gardens**, recently redeveloped, or take one of the cliff lifts back to St Nicholas Cliff.

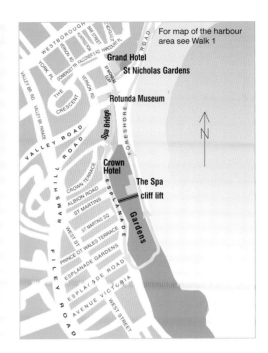

3. North Bay

Start at Mulgrave Place, near St Mary's Church, from which both bays can be seen. Turn left along the cliff top, admiring the views of the North Bay and of the buildings on Rutland Terrace and Blenheim Terrace. Walk down Albert Road to Royal Albert Drive and head north towards the **Corner Complex**, formerly the **Corner Café**. Walk alongside the **beach bungalows** to **Scalby Mills**, and see the modern **Sea Life Centre**, before heading up to the station and taking the **miniature railway** to Peasholm Station. On the way you will pass through **Northstead Manor Gardens**, which contains the **Open Air Theatre**. Cross the road to **Peasholm Park**, originating in the Edwardian period but much developed since, and then walk uphill on Victoria Park to the Alexandra Bowls Centre, built on the site of the **Floral Hall**, where entertainments were staged for many decades. Finally, stroll along North Marine Road, passing the **cricket ground**, towards the town centre.

Acknowledgements

The publication of this book would not have been possible without the generous grant from the Local Heritage Initiative, a partnership between the Countryside Agency, the Heritage Lottery Fund and Nationwide Building Society.

The photographs of Broadway on p. 11, Newborough Gate on p. 15, damage to the Old Town on pp. 16–17, and the pill box on p. 19 are reproduced by kind permission of Scarborough Borough Council. The photographs of the Scarborough Ware water jug on p. 44 and the portrait of H.B. Carter by George Green on p. 68 are reproduced by kind permission of Scarborough Museums & Gallery, Scarborough Borough Council. The aerial photographs of castle hill on p. 7 and the Roman watchtower on p. 13 are reproduced by kind permission of Anthony Crawshaw. The drawings of the layout of the Old Town and the reconstruction of St Mary's are reproduced by kind permission of David Pearson. The medieval recipe on p. 21 from *Recipes of Old England: Three Centuries of English Cooking* (1973), modernised by Bernard Bessunger, is reproduced by kind permission of David & Charles.

The undated colour postcard of the Scarborough Open Air Theatre on p. 56 derives from a 1938 LNER poster by Frank Mason (1876-1965), printed by E.T. Dennis & Sons; the undated postcard on p. 63 showing a photograph of the production of *Annie Get Your Gun* is the copyright of H.O. Taylor; the map of Scarborough's attractions on pp. 2–3 is taken from *A Guide to Scarborough* (undated), published by H.O. Taylor Ltd.

Many of the illustrations appearing in this book come from the archives held in the Local Studies Room of the Scarborough Public Library, which kindly allowed us to photograph the following: the advertisements on pp. 42-47 from *A Directory of Scarborough* (1892), *Crosby's Scarborough Guide* (1856) and *Visitors and Residents Directory and Gazetteer of Scarborough* (1855); the prints of 'The Breakfast' on p. 52, 'The Warm Bath' and 'The Terrace' on p. 54, 'The Theatre' on p. 65, 'The Bookshop' on p. 66, and 'The Ballroom' on p. 69 from *Poetical Sketches of Scarborough* (1813) by J. Green and T. Rowlandson; W. Tindall's drawing of The Crescent on p. 10; the watercolour of the Three Mariners public house (1911) by W. King on p. 23; the photograph of Tindall's shipyard on p. 26; the drawing of Trinity House on p. 25 and the engraving of 'The Hall of the Mechanics Institute' on p. 67 from *Theakston's Guide to Scarborough* (1861); the woodprint of the 'Spaw' from *The Scarborough Guide* (1815) by Baynes and Carrall on p. 49; the engraving of Dicky Dickinson from *A Journey from London to Scarborough in Several Letters* (Clark, 1734) on p. 48; the 'Cliff and Terrace, Scarbro. as improved in 1829' engraving by J. Greenwood on p. 53; 'The Museum and Cliff Bridge' colour print on p. 1 and p. 64; the photographs of the Hannay Bible on p. 32 and Pritchard's Band in 1870 on p. 69 from *The History of Scarborough* (1931) edited by A. Rowntree.

Thanks to the Scarborough Museums & Gallery for allowing us to photograph J.W. Carmichaels's *Scarborough from the Sea* (1867) used on the cover and the Mote Stone on p. 19. Grateful thanks to Tony Mills, vicar of St Martin-on-the-Hill, for allowing us to photograph the pulpit on p. 33. Max Payne provided the photograph of the Scotch fisher lasses on p. 22 and Simon Smith provided us with images of the damaged lighthouse on p. 27 on CD ROM. We are grateful to the British Library for providing us with a CD ROM of the view of the town in 1538 on p. 6 and p. 37.

Robert Updegraff drew the maps on p. 20, p. 38 and pp. 70-71 and took the photographs on p. 28, p. 31 and p. 35, the copyright to which belongs to the Scarborough Archaeological and Historical Society. Geoff Wood took the photographs on p. 9, p. 12, p. 39, p. 40, p. 41 and p. 47, the copyright to which is owned by the Society. Unless otherwise indicated, the copyrights to all illustrations in the book are the property of the Scarborough Archaeological and Historical Society.

The Scarborough Archaeological and Historical Society has attempted to contact copyright owners of artwork reproduced in this book and it welcomes queries from those not acknowledged above. Queries should be sent to The Secretary, SAHS, 10 Westbourne Park, Scarborough YO12 4AT.